iPhone SE 2020 user guide

BY

Piers N.Lowe

DISCLAIMER:

The information contained in this book is for educational purposes only. All efforts have been executed to present accurate, reliable, and up to date information. No warranties of any kind are implied. The contents from this book are from various sources. Please consult a licensed professional before attempting any techniques contained herein.

By reading this document, the reader agrees that under no circumstances is the author responsible for any losses, direct or indirect, which are incurred as a result of the information contained in this book including errors, omissions, and inaccuracy.

Table of Contents

Introduction

Over the years, Apple has set a standard for all other companies to follow in terms of smartphone designs. With this in mind, Apple introduced the iPhone SE in April 2020.

The iPhone SE comes in black and white (PRODUCT) RED, made with glass on the front and back, and a color-matched aluminum strip.

It supports wireless charging and is waterproof and dustproof in accordance with

IP67, so it is protected from accidental spills, and even water.

The top bezel has a 7- megapixel camera and a microphone on the front, while the bottom frame has a Touch ID Home button for biometric authentication using fingerprint.

In terms of battery life, the iPhone SE gets 13 hours for video, eight hours for video, and 40 hours for audio.

The iPhone SE does not have a U1 chip, but it supports the latest, fastest Wi-Fi protocols, Wi-Fi 6, Bluetooth 5 with 2x2 MIMO and Gigabit LTE.

Design

The iPhone SE 2020, has a screen display that is around 4.7-inches.Which has thick bezels at its top and bottom.

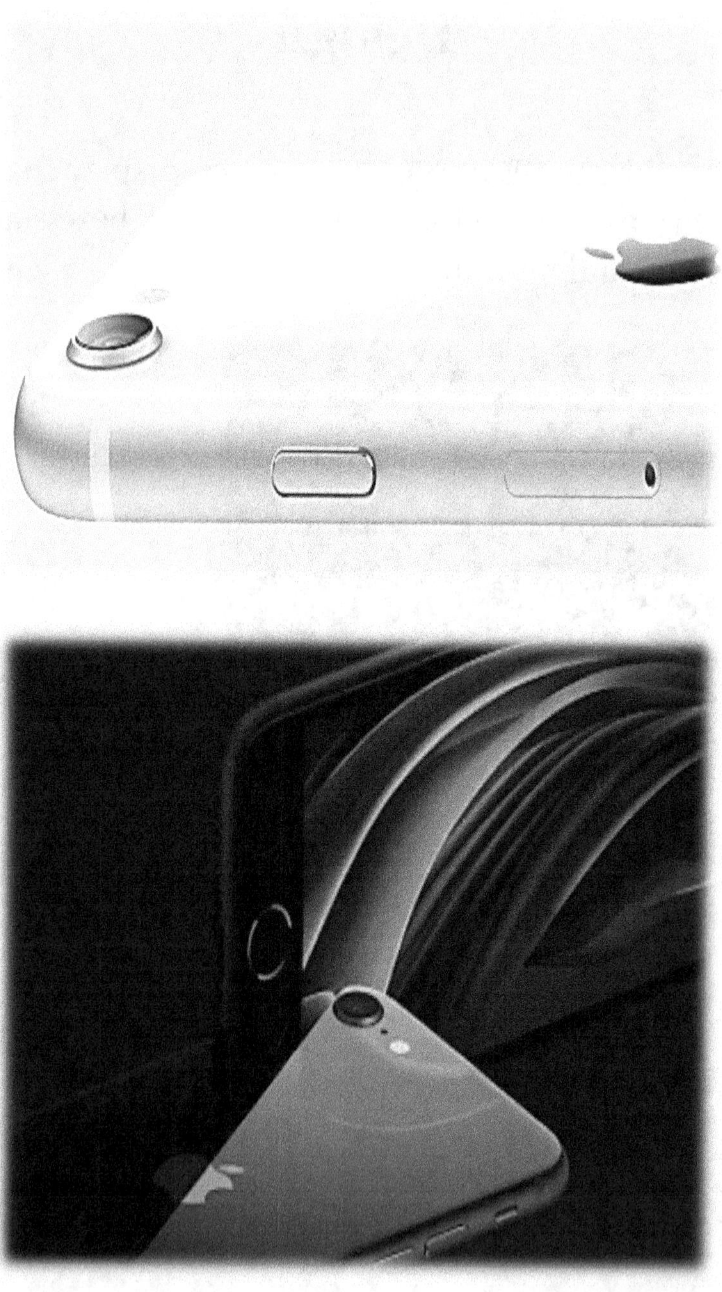

The iPhone SE 2020 is around 138.4 mm in height, 67.3 mm in width, and 7.3 mm in thickness and weighs 5.22 ounces

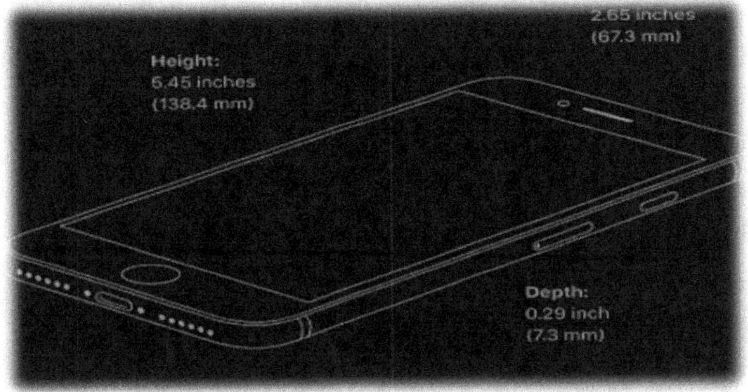

The iPhone SE comes in white, gray, blue (PRODUCT) RED version with a bright red glass back.

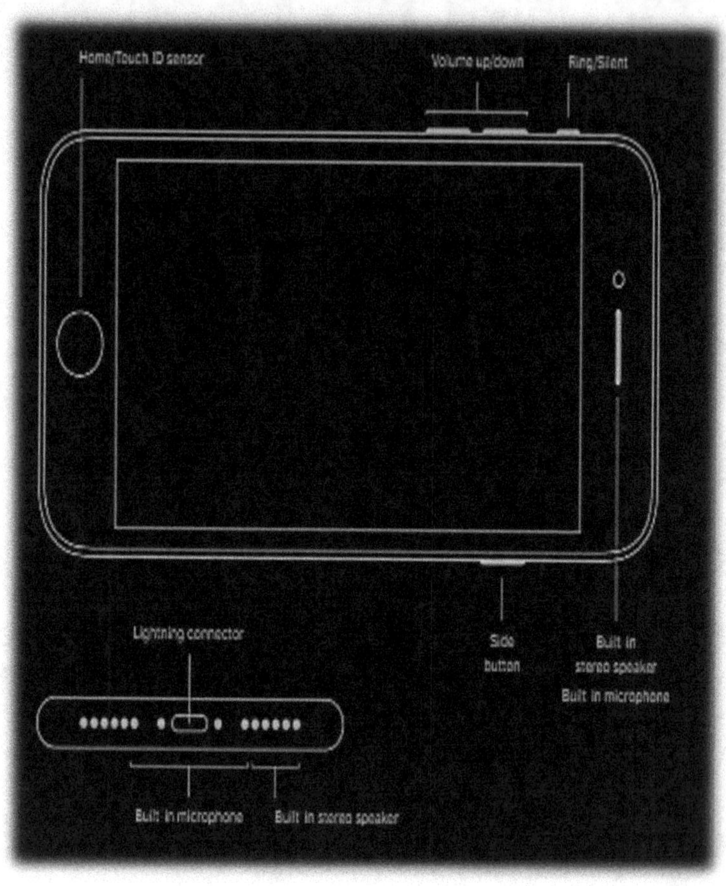
Home/Touch ID sensor
Volume up/down
Ring/Silent
Lightning connector
Side
button
Built in
stereo speaker
Built in microphone
Built in microphone
Built in stereo speaker

Display

The iPhone SE is similar to the 4.7-inch screen used in the iPhone 8, with resolutions ranging from 1,334 to 750, 326 pixels per inch, and 1,400: 1.Contrast ratio.

Its genuine P3 color, multi-touch, with wide color support, max brightness 625 nits.

True Tone takes advantage of an ambient light sensor to detect the light in the room and adjust the color temperature and intensity to make more light adjustments.

Haptic touch

The iPhone SE 2020 is equipped with a Haptic touch which works just like the 3D touch. Although it is a remarkable feature, it is not sensitive to pressure.

The Haptic touch is used to perform many actions which may include granting instant access to Quick Actions on the Home screen of your iPhone.

To get preview links on Safari and to do other tasks such as enabling flash on lock screen.

The Haptic Touch on the iPhone SE 2020 does not function on the lock screen or at the notification center.

To power the iPhone SE 2020 is an A13 Bionic chip. With an eight-core neural motor that performs real-time image and video analysis like never before. Machine learning accelerator CPUs are six times faster and perform more than 1 trillion times per second.

Camera

The iPhone SE is equipped with a single-lens rear camera. With a 12-megapixel wide-angle camera which has optical image stabilization, the iPhone SE 2020 is able to capture images with a wider color resolution, which allows the camera to focus on details.

The iPhone SE lacks an optical zoom support as well as Night mode.

The iPhone SE 2020 supports portrait mode despite lacking two cameras as well as support for portrait exposure and depth control. With QuickTake Video, the iPhone SE 2020 gives users the freedom to quickly capture a video by touching the camera button.

00:00:03

iPhone SE 2020 BASICS

In this section, we will cover the basic things you need to get started with your iPhone SE 2020.

How to turn on your iPhone SE

Turning on your iPhone is probably the easiest thing you will ever do. To switch it on, push and hold the side button of your iPhone for few seconds.

The next step is to set up your iPhone using an internet connection which could be a Wi-Fi network or a cellular data service.

Now, to set up your iPhone SE 2020 press Set Manually and then follow the next steps that will show on your screen. If you previously own an iPhone that uses iOS 11 and later, or an iPad that uses iPadOS 13 or later, you can automatically set up your iPhone SE using Quick Start which copies your settings, iCloud Keychain and others.

This step is easy as it involves bringing both devices close and then following the steps that will appear on the screen.

Setting up your iPhone SE cellular service

Your iPhone SE needs a cellular connection from a SIM from a carrier.

- *Insert a paper clip into the small hole in the SIM tray and push in the shelf to the right of your iPhone, and remove the tray.*

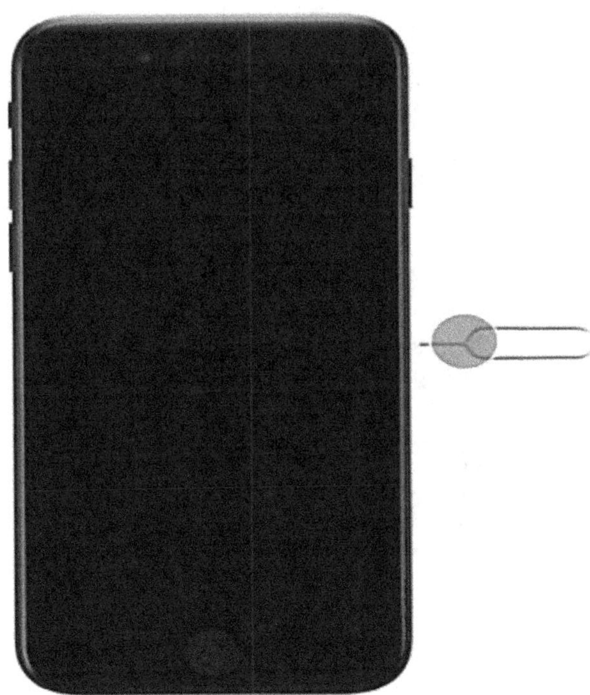

- *Remove the shelf from the iPhone.*

- *Place the nano SIM on the shelf. The angle determines the correct setting.*
- *Put the shelf back into the iPhone.*

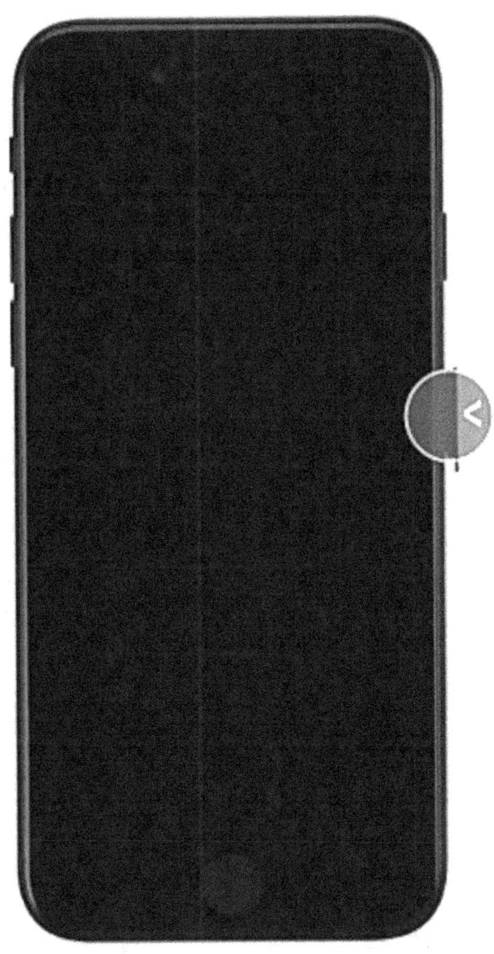

Set up your mobile service plan using ESIM.

- *Go to Settings> Cell Phone and click Add Cell Plan.*

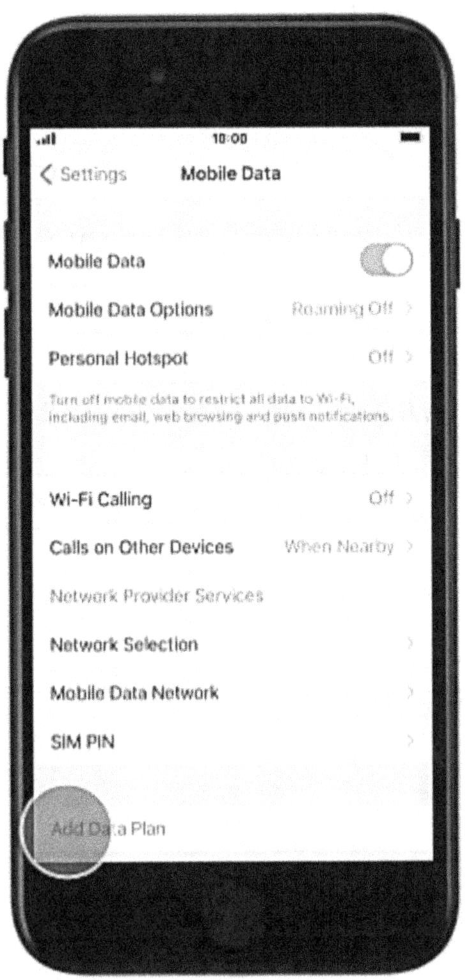

- *To connect your iPhone to a Wi-Fi network, simply open settings and then navigate to Wi-Fi to turn it on.*

- *To join a private hotspot, open the Settings app and then scroll to Wi-Fi, choose the name of the hotspot to share with your device.*
- *If you want to enter a passcode on your iPhone, enter the passcode shown in Settings> Cell> Private hotspot on the private hotspot sharing device.*

Connect your iPhone to a cellular network.

If you don't have a Wi-Fi network, your iPhone will automatically connect to your carrier's cellular network, and if your iPhone doesn't, check the following.

- *Make sure your SIM is active and unlocked.*
- *Open settings and then navigate to Mobile and ensure your data is turned on.*

Dark mode

Dark mode allows the iPhone to experience dark tones in low light environments.

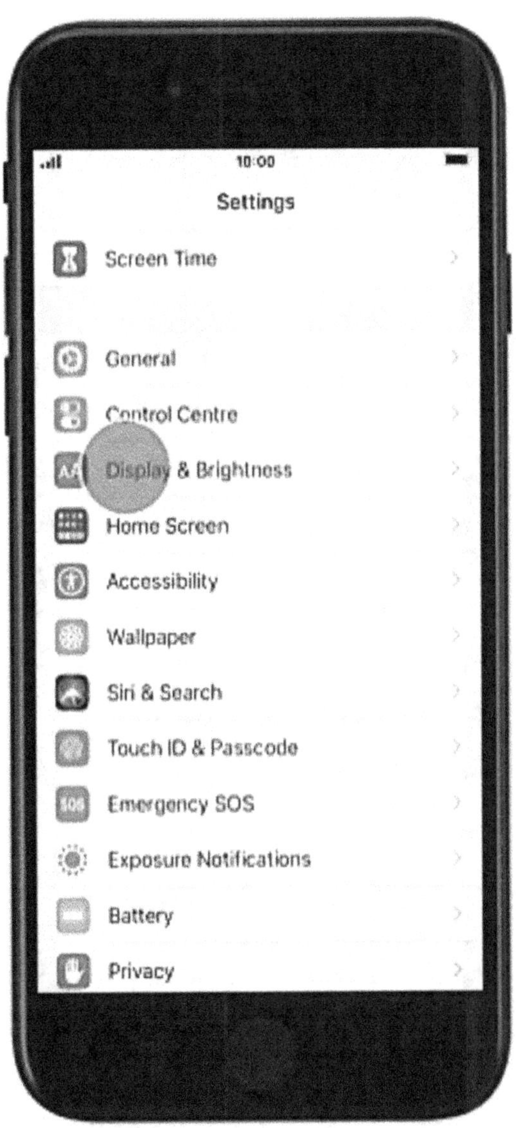
10:00
Settings
Screen Time
General
Control Centre
Display & Brightness
Home Screen
Accessibility
Wallpaper
Siri & Search
Touch ID & Passcode
Emergency SOS
Exposure Notifications
Battery
Privacy

10:00
Settings   Display & Brightness
APPEARANCE
09:41
09:41
Light
Dark
Automatic
BRIGHTNESS
True Tone
Automatically adapt iPhone display based on ambient lighting conditions to make colours appear consistent in different environments.
Night Shift   Off

To turn on dark mode, simply open the control center and the hold the brightness button, and then press the Appearance button.

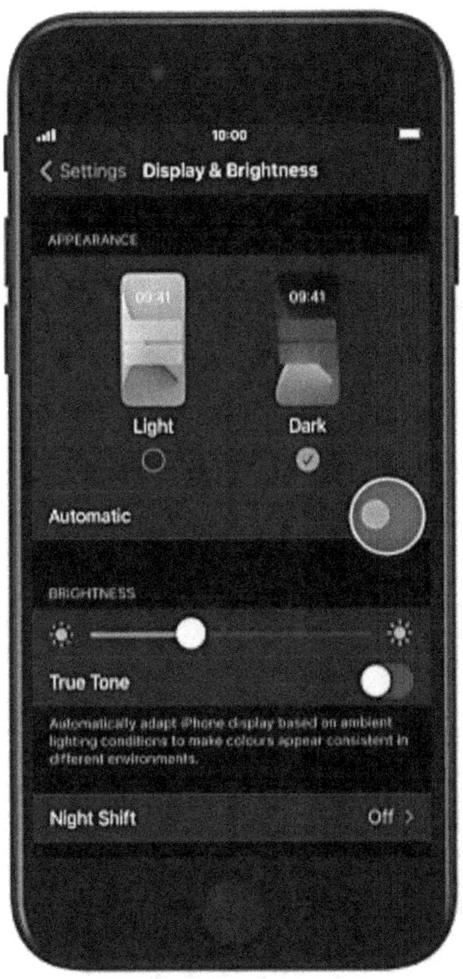

To schedule your iPhone to automatically turn dark mode on and off, go to Settings and then

Display and brightness to select the automatically turn on option.

Choose sunset or set the set time for sunrise.

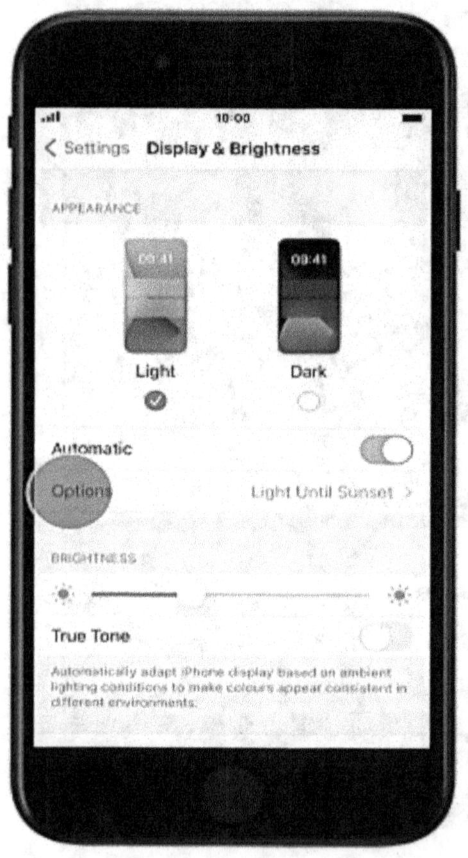

If you select the Sunset to Sunrise option, the iPhone will determine your time of night using your time and geographic location information.

Adjust the screen brightness manually

To dim or brighten the iPhone screen, simply open the control center by swiping on your home screen and then dragging the brightness slider.

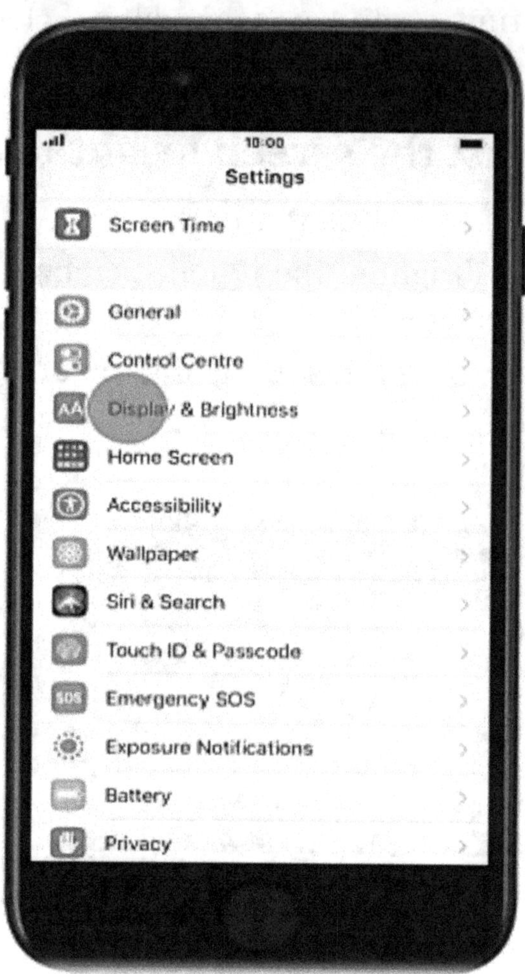
10:00
Settings
Screen Time
General
Control Centre
Display & Brightness
Home Screen
Accessibility
Wallpaper
Siri & Search
Touch ID & Passcode
Emergency SOS
Exposure Notifications
Battery
Privacy

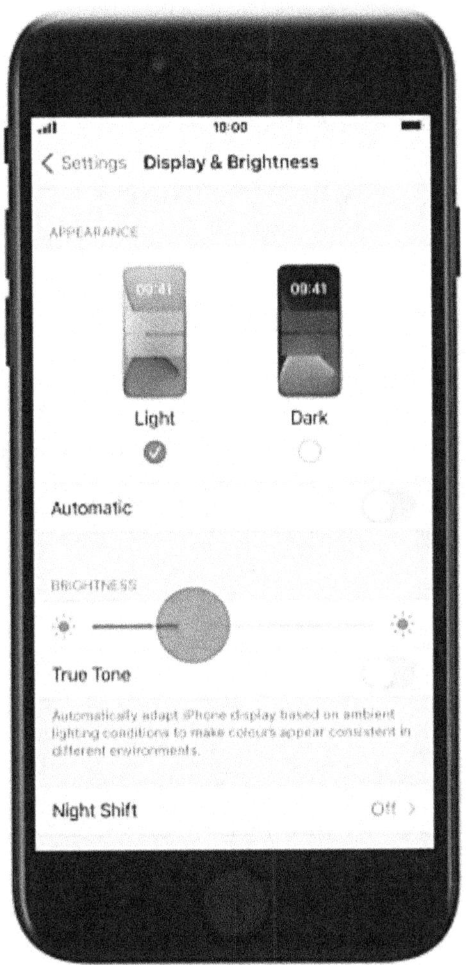

You can turn on Night shift on your iPhone SE by opening   Settings and then navigating to **Display & Brightness> Night Shift**, and then schedule the time.

To adjust Night Shift's color balance, drag the slider below the color temperature to the warm or cool end of the spectrum.

And then choose Sunset to Sunrise or Order Schedule.

If you choose a custom schedule, click Options to schedule Night Shift on and off.

If you choose the sunset to sunrise option, iPhone uses your time and location data to assign you night time.

Create a screen record

You can record screenshots and receive audio on your iPhone.

Go to Settings> Control Center and click the Insert Screen Recorder button next to Screen Recording.

Open the control center hit the screen record button and wait three seconds to count.

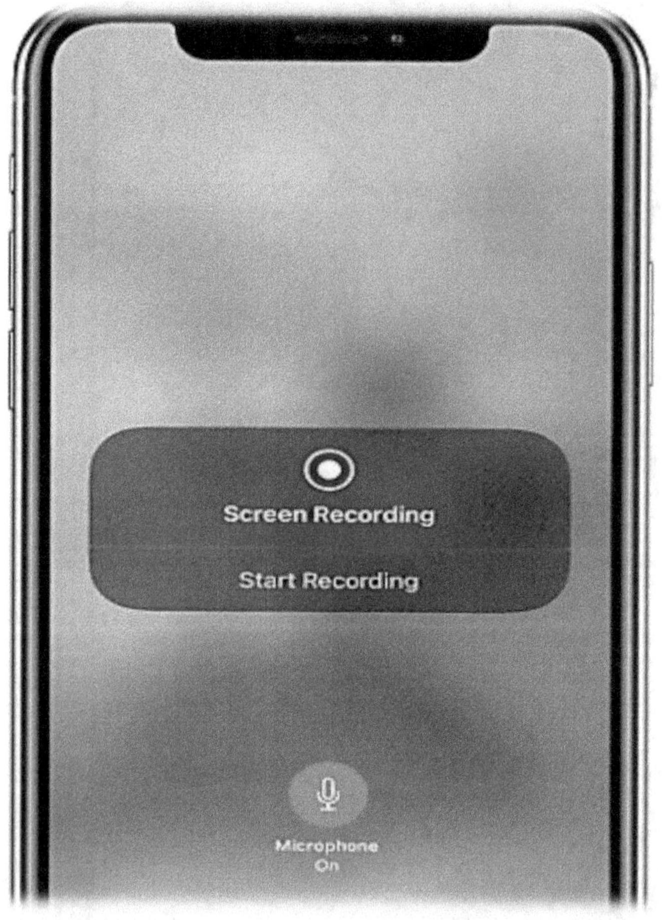

To stop recording, open Control Center and press the selected screen record button or the red status bar at the top of the screen to stop recording.

Change lock screen on iPhone

Many apps give it a different look when you rotate your iPhone.

You can lock your iPhone without changing the orientation of the screen when you rotate it.

Open Control Center, then click the lock direction.

How to set a Wallpaper

To set wallpaper, simply open the settings app and the scroll to Wallpaper and then choose new Wallpaper.

You can choose customized wallpapers or you can use your picture as wallpaper which you can use as the lock screen or the home screen.

Choose a New Wallpaper

Dark Appearance Dims Wallpaper

When Dark Appearance is on, iPhone will dim your wallpaper depending on your ambient light.

Dynamic wallpaper and perspective zoom are disabled when Low Power Mode is on.

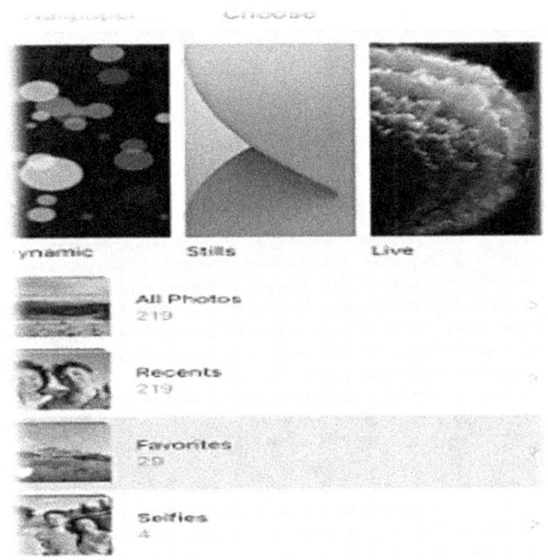

You can also set live image as lock screen wallpaper.

Select Settings> Wallpaper> New Wallpaper.

Press live and select the image directly.

Press the Live Photos album and select a Live Photo.

Turn on Do not disturb feature

This feature quickly turns off your iPhone's notification sound. Open Control Center, click the Do Not Disturb icon, and turn on Do Not Disturb mode.

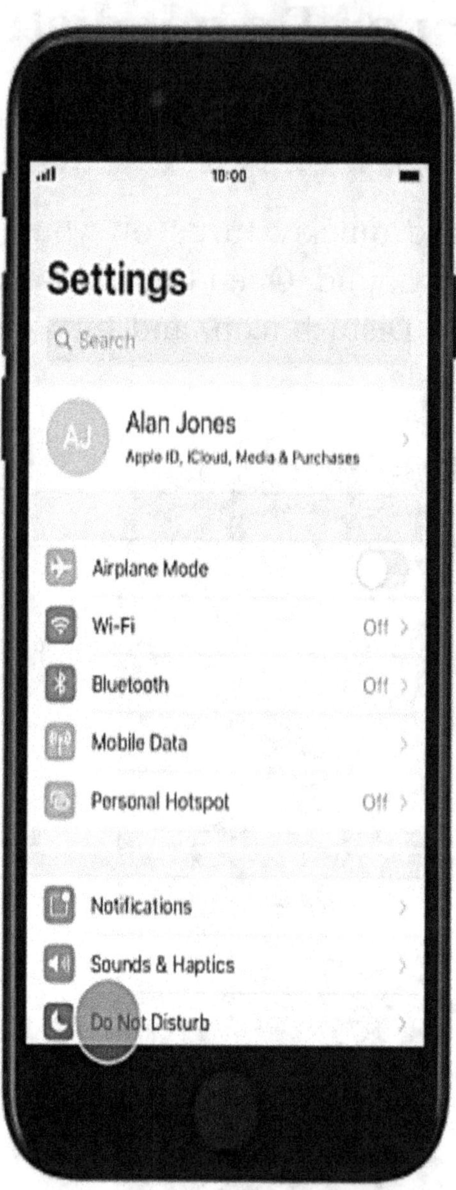
10:00
Settings
Search
AJ
Alan Jones
Apple ID, iCloud, Media & Purchases
Airplane Mode
Wi-Fi
Off
Bluetooth
Off
Mobile Data
Personal Hotspot
Off
Notifications
Sounds & Haptics
Do Not Disturb

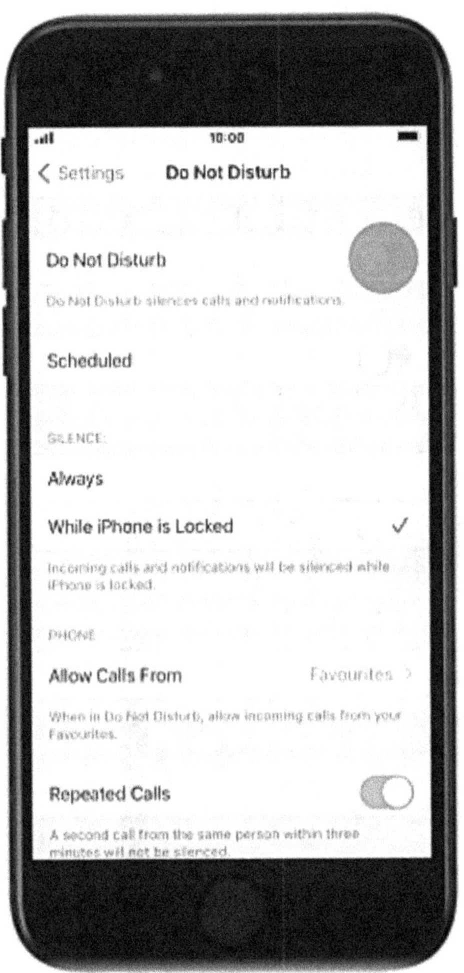

You can also fix an end time for the Don Not Disturb feature by pressing and holding the icon in Control Center and then selecting an option.

You can also click Schedule, open schedule settings, and set start and end times.

Make a quiet schedule

Go to Settings> Do Not Disturb Mode.

Open schedule settings and set the start and end times for the silent time.

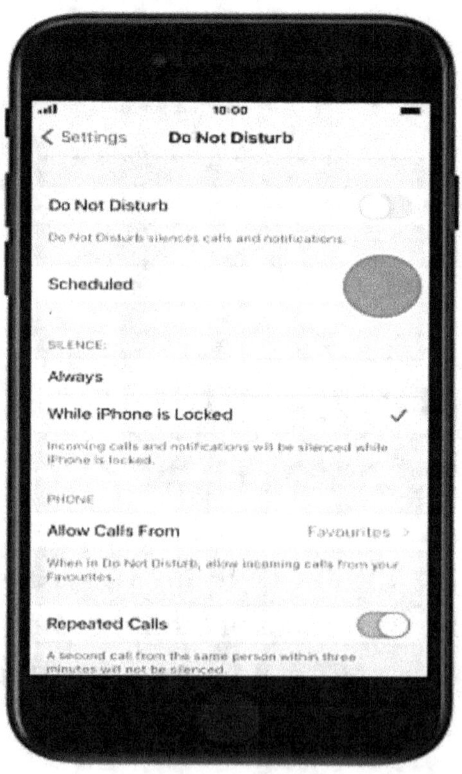

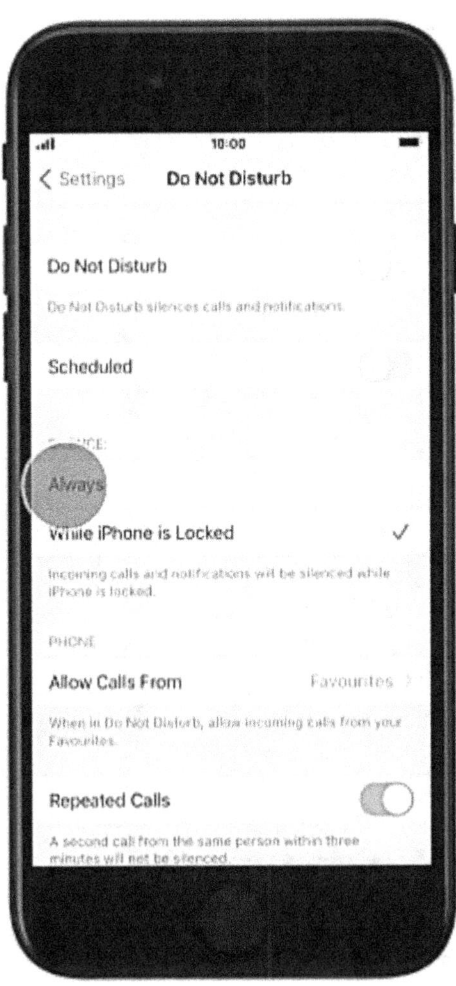

10:00
< Settings   Do Not Disturb
Do Not Disturb
Do Not Disturb silences calls and notifications.
Scheduled
SILENCE:
Always
While iPhone is Locked
Incoming calls and notifications will be silenced while iPhone is locked.
PHONE
Allow Calls From   Favourites
When in Do Not Disturb, allow incoming calls from your Favourites.
Repeated Calls
A second call from the same person within three minutes will not be silenced.

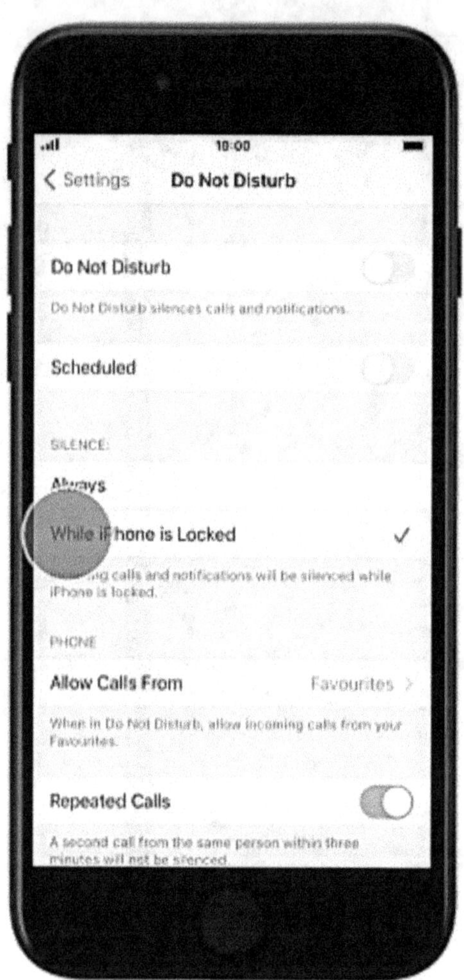

10:00
< Settings   Do Not Disturb
Do Not Disturb
Do Not Disturb silences calls and notifications.
Scheduled
SILENCE:
Always
While iPhone is Locked
Incoming calls and notifications will be silenced while iPhone is locked.
PHONE
Allow Calls From   Favourites >
When in Do Not Disturb, allow incoming calls from your Favourites.
Repeated Calls
A second call from the same person within three minutes will not be silenced.

Taking photos

What's an iPhone without taking pictures? The iPhone is very useful for taking nice and sharp photos.

To take a photo with your iPhone camera, simply open the camera app and then tap the shutter button.

00:00:00
HD · 30
SLO·MO
VIDEO
PHOTO
PORTRAIT

To make a video or to see other photo options, simply swipe to the left or the right.

SLO-MO
VIDEO
PHOTO
PORTRAIT
PANO

To set a timer for your camera, simply press the control button and then press the timer button.

To take a selfie, simply switch to the front camera by pressing the camera chooser button. The next step is to place the iPhone in your front with an out stretched arm and then press the shutter.

How to Set up FaceTime

With the FaceTime app, you can call friends and loved ones with video or audio calls.

To make a FaceTime call, simply go to settings and then scroll to FaceTime to switch it on.

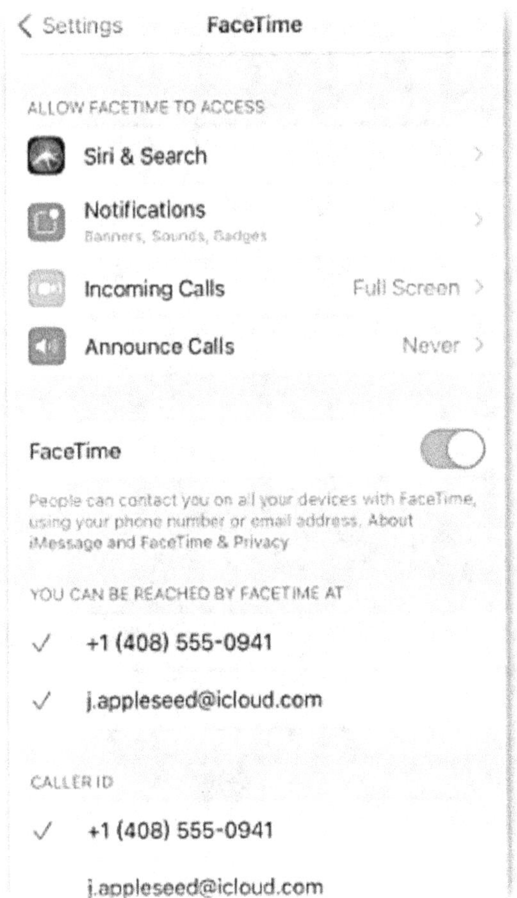

The next step is to open the FaceTime app and then then enter your Apple ID phone number or email address to use FaceTime.

To call a contact, press the add button and then enter the name or number you want to call in the input field above, then click Video to Make Video or Audio Call to FaceTime Audio.

Set up messages on iPhone

In the messaging app, you can send messages in the form of text / text messages to people using Wi-Fi or cellular service or using iMessage. Messages sent and received using your iMessage are not included in the SMS / MMS fee on your messaging plan.

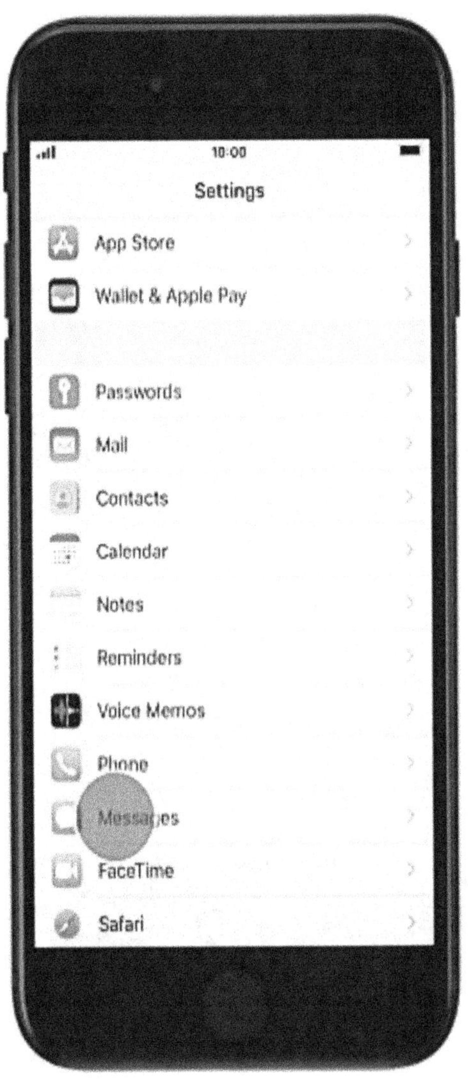

IMessage messages appear as blue foam, SMS / MMS messages appear in green foam.

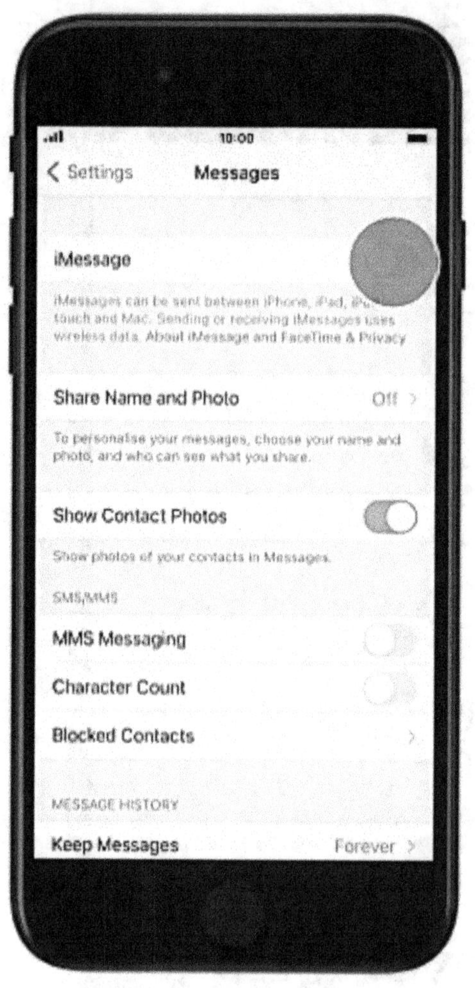

To sign in to iMessage, open the settings app and then navigate to iMessages to turn it on.

With Continuity, all SMS / MMS messages sent and received on your iPhone will be displayed on your other iOS devices and Macs.

Send and receive messages on iPhone

You can send and receive messages, photos, videos, and audio messages using the messaging app.

Edit
Messages
Search

Enter a phone number, contact name, or Apple ID for each recipient you want to send a message to.

10:00
New Message
Cancel
To: Zoe Taylor
Text Message

Using Safari

With Safari, you can quickly browse the web, add webpages to your reading list, and then quickly add reading icons and pages to your home page.

You can easily navigate to any web page with just a few clicks.

See more on page: Move your iPhone horizontally.

Refresh the page: Click the Reload button next to an address in the search field.

Share link: Click the Share button.

Change screen font size and website settings.

Use the menu to reduce the message size, go to the Viewer menu, specify privacy restrictions, and view.

Adjust the font size: Click A to expand the font or click A to decrease the font size.

View pages without ads or navigation menus: Click Show Reader View.

Hide the search field: Click Hide Toolbar.

View desktop version of the web page: Click the option to request a desktop website.

You can preview links by clicking on them in Safari without opening the page. Please preview or choose another option to open the link.

To view the webpage in another language, click the Website radio button and click the Translate button.

Screen Time

This feature shows you how long you use your iPhone, and the time you spend on each app.

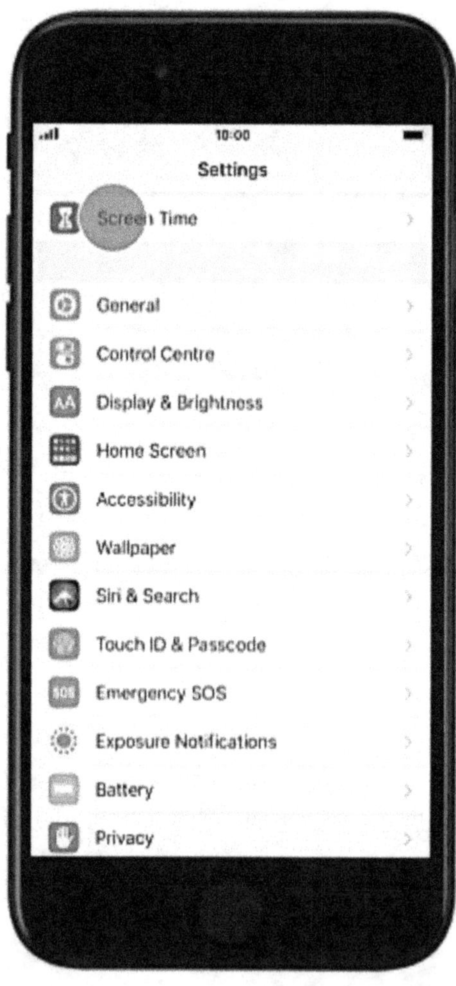

When you set your Screen Time, it will begin generating usage descriptions for your device. i.e. it gives info on how much time you spend on an app, either a social media app, an entertainment app, etc. It also shows overused apps.

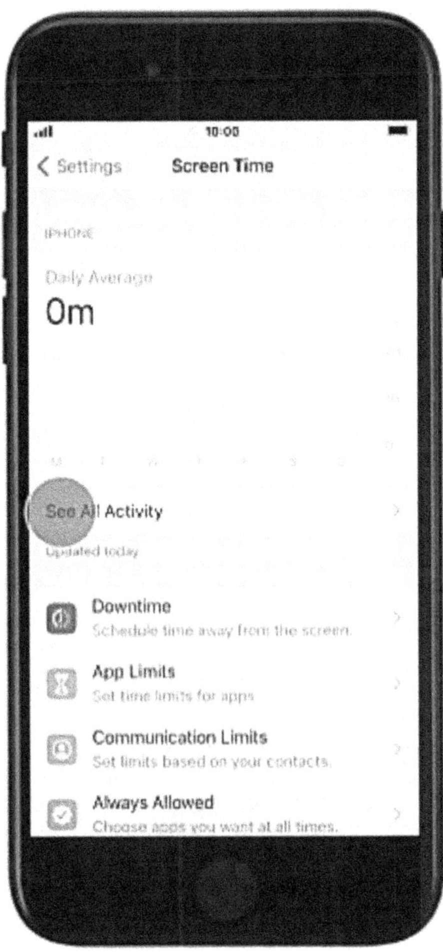

How often do you pick up your device, which apps do you use, or in other words, how many times did you use each app after you picked up your device?

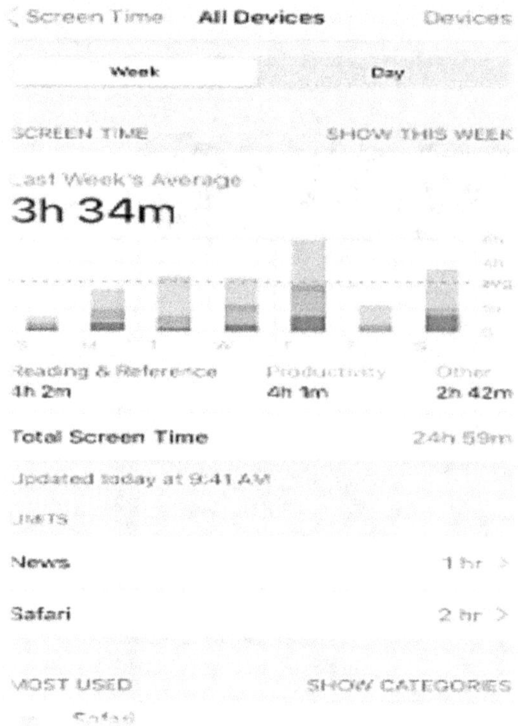

You can click on each application.

When setting the display time, you can see a summary in the overview in Settings> Show time> View all events.

SECURITY

To prevent unauthorized people gaining access to the files and data on your iPhone, you have to keep it secured. We will show you ways on how to keep your iPhone safe and secured.

Set a passcode

The first step to protect your iPhone is to set a secure passcode you can easily remember.

Open Settings and then tap Touch ID and Passcode. Then you turn the passcode on.

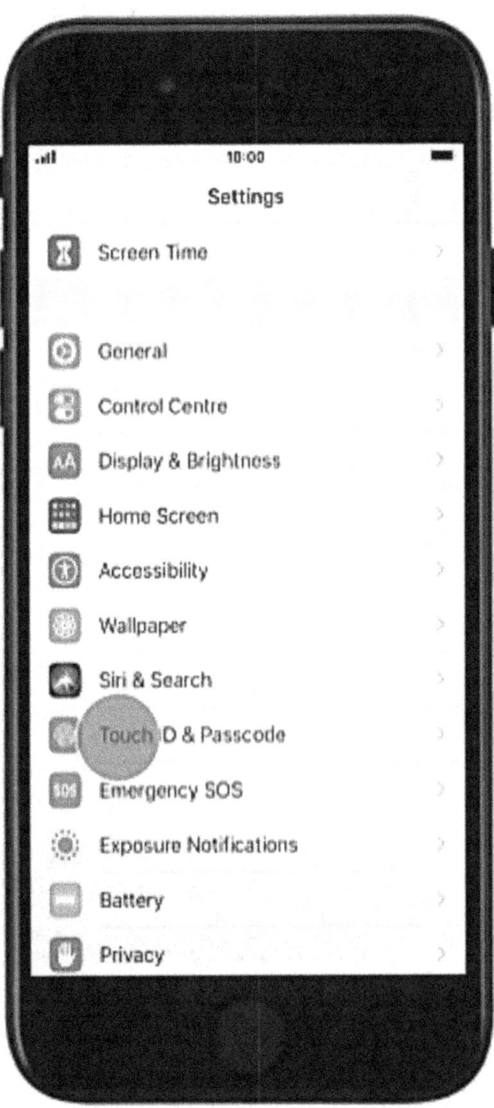
10:00
Settings
Screen Time
General
Control Centre
Display & Brightness
Home Screen
Accessibility
Wallpaper
Siri & Search
Touch ID & Passcode
Emergency SOS
Exposure Notifications
Battery
Privacy

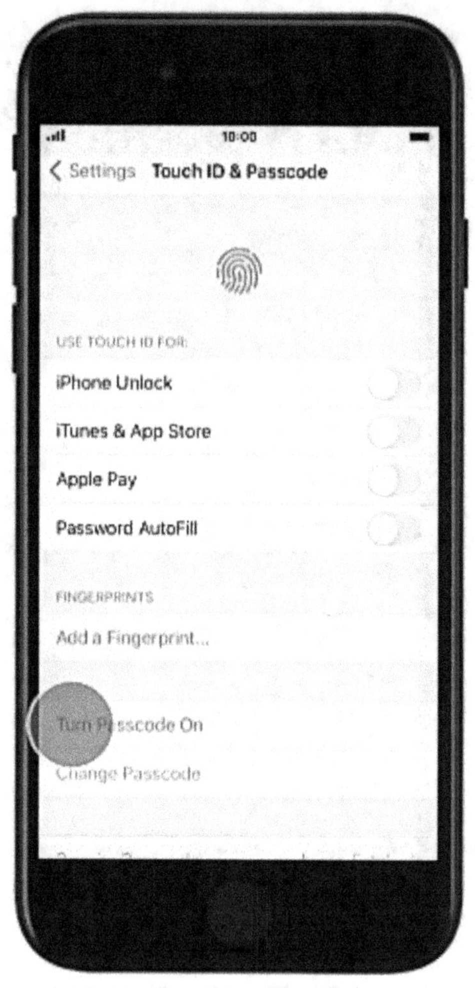

After setting a passcode, you can also set Touch ID for extra security.

Reset the passcode

You are locked out of your iPhone if you input the wrong Passcode

To reset a passcode when you can't remember it, you can erase your phone if you have a backup to set a new passcode.

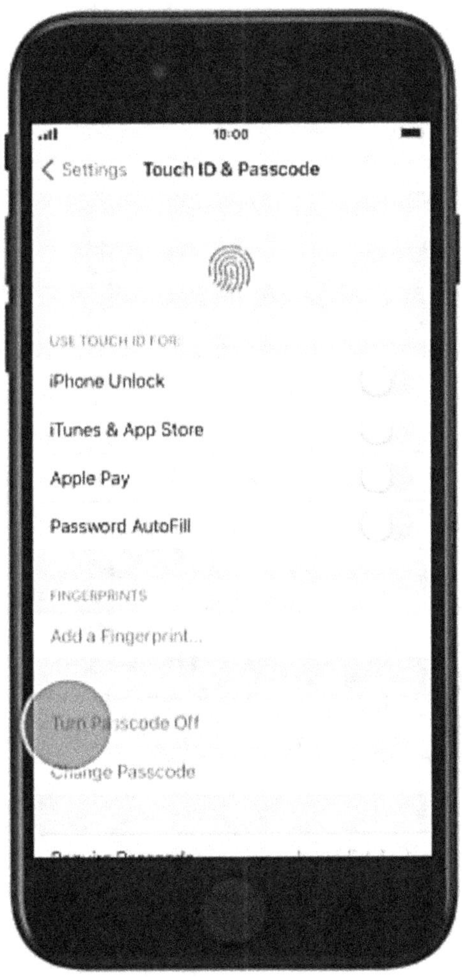

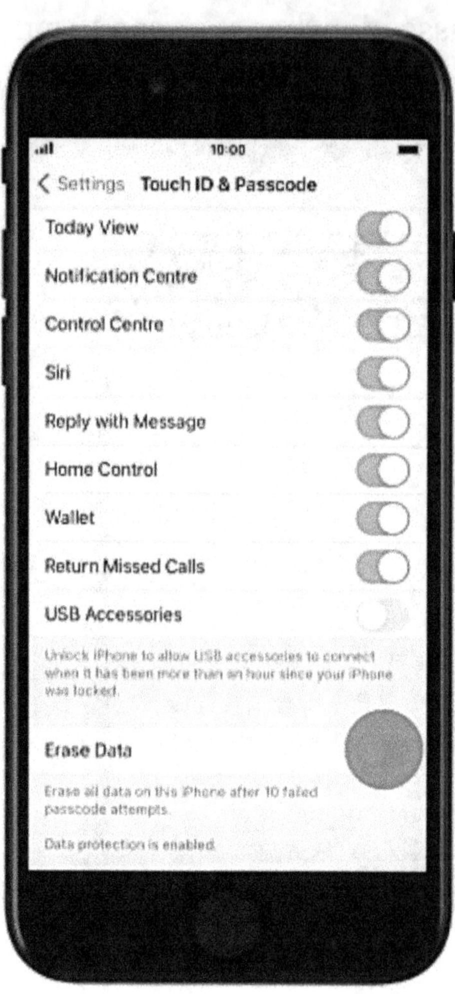

10:00
Settings   Touch ID & Passcode
Today View
Notification Centre
Control Centre
Siri
Reply with Message
Home Control
Wallet
Return Missed Calls
USB Accessories
Unlock iPhone to allow USB accessories to connect when it has been more than an hour since your iPhone was locked.
Erase Data
Erase all data on this iPhone after 10 failed passcode attempts.
Data protection is enabled.

Set up Touch ID on iPhone

To set up touch ID on your phone, simply open settings and then navigate to Touch ID & Passcode, and then follow on screen instructions.

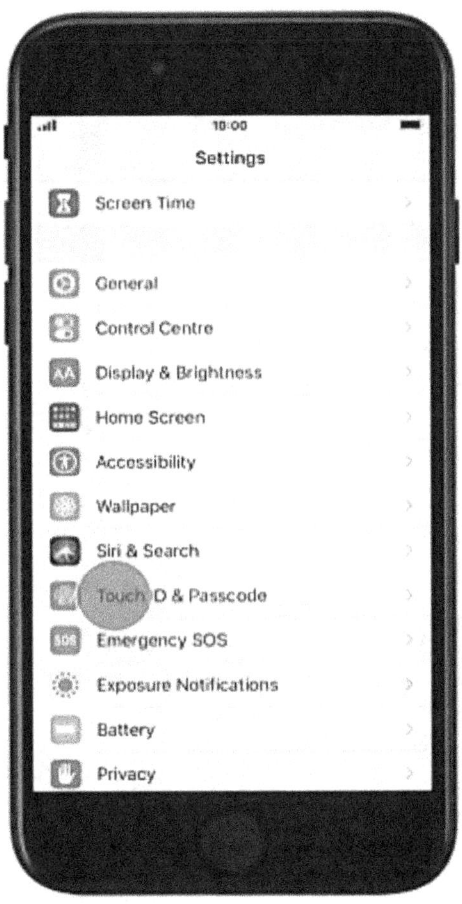

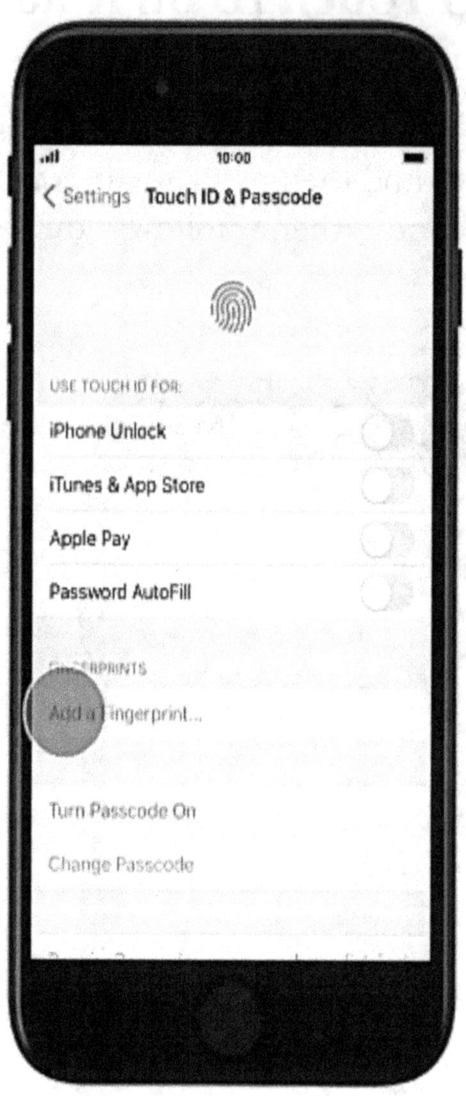
10:00
Settings   Touch ID & Passcode
USE TOUCH ID FOR:
iPhone Unlock
iTunes & App Store
Apple Pay
Password AutoFill
FINGERPRINTS
Add a Fingerprint...
Turn Passcode On
Change Passcode

10:00
Cancel
Adjust Your Grip
Keep going to capture the edges
of your print.
Continue

10:00
Complete
Touch ID is ready. Your print can be used
for unlocking your iPhone.
Continue

10:00
Settings   Touch ID & Passcode
USE TOUCH ID FOR:
iPhone Unlock
iTunes & App Store
Apple Pay
Password AutoFill
FINGERPRINTS
Finger 1
Add a Fingerprint...
Turn Passcode Off
Change Passcode

How to update iOS on iPhone

Updating to the latest iOS will keep your information and settings unchanged.

Before upgrading, either back up your iPhone automatically or manually back up your device.

Automatically update iPhone

To automatically update your iPhone, open settings and then press General, and then press Software Update.

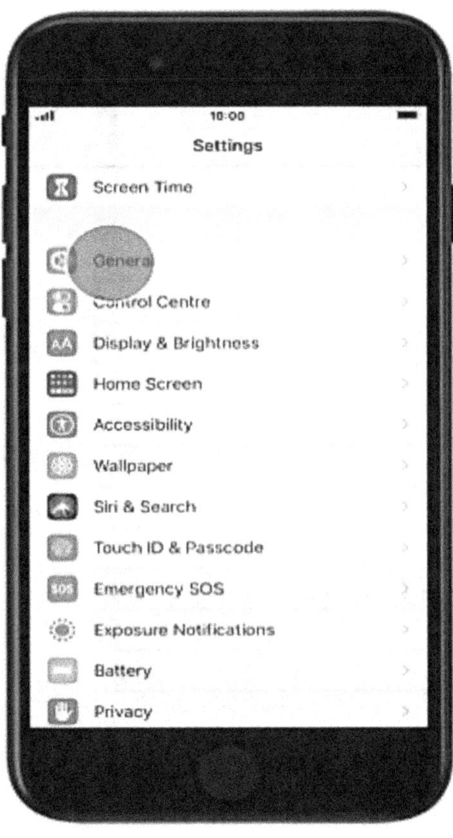

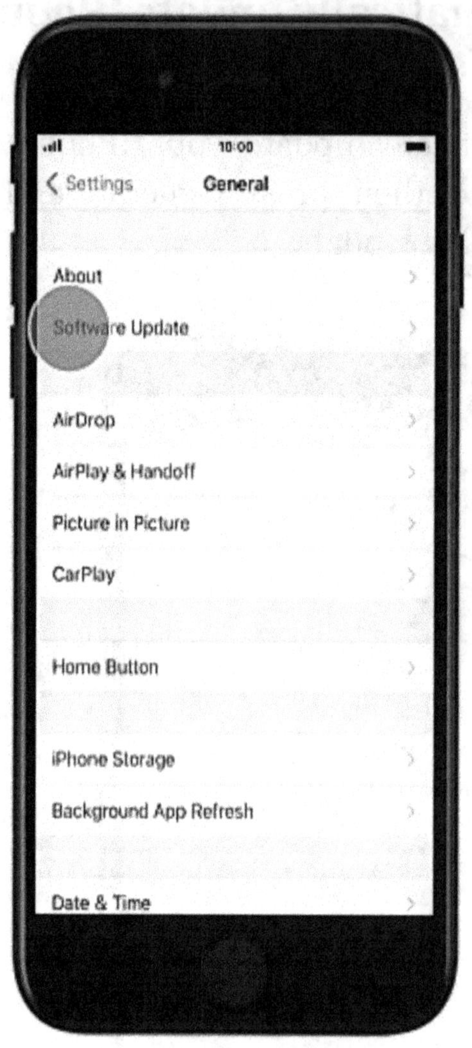

Your iPhone automatically updates its software when a new update is available.

Manually update the iPhone

To manually update your iPhone, open Settings and then navigate to General and then press Software Update.

Your current iOS version will be displayed and then if any update is available, it informs you.

INDEX

www.ingramcontent.com/pod-product-compliance
Lightning Source LLC
Chambersburg PA
CBHW071940120726
48001CB00005B/1975